TAMESIDE LIBRARIES

3 8016 0200 32944   KT-425-522

www. Tameside .gov.uk

HYDE LIBRARY

WITHDRAWN FROM
TAMESIDE LIBRARIES

TRACEY TURNER

STAT ATTACK!

CRAZY CARS

LONDON·SYDNEY

Franklin Watts
First published in Great Britain in 2015 by
The Watts Publishing Group

Copyright © Tracey Turner 2015

The author has asserted her rights in accordance
with the Copyright, Designs and Patents Act, 1988.

All rights reserved.

Credits
Series editor: Adrian Cole
Series designer: Matt Lilly
Art direction: Peter Scoulding
Photo acknowledgements:
AFP/Getty Images: 6t. Michael Ballard/Social region: 22bl. Folco
Banfi/Dreamstime: 9br. bankerwin/Shutterstock: 23c. Robert
Paul van Beet/Shutterstock: 22br. Phillip Bird LRPS BPAGB/
Shutterstock: 27cb, 31b. Darren Brode/Shutterstock: 23b. Walter
Cattaneo/Dreamstime: 28cl. Birsem Cebeci/Shutterstock: 27c.
Chameleon Eyes/Shutterstock: 16c. David Cooper/Getty Images:
29c. Dauer cars: 19t. Jeremy Davey/© SSC Programme Ltd:
9b. Alan Dyer/Shutterstock: 16b. Max Earey/Dreamstime: 27b.
ebilnorge.no/wikimedia commons: 29t. efecreata mediagoup/
Shutterstock: 25b. elwynn/Shutterstock: 5cr. Essen Motor
Show: 10b. Fabinus 08/Dreamstime: 29b. Ferret: 21bl. Fingerhut/
Shutterstock: 18cl. Funny Solutions Studio/Shutterstock: 5cl.
Nate Hawkbaker/wikimedia commons: 18cr. Daniel Huerlimann-
BEELDE/Shutterstock: 21br. Kandi: 28cr. Keystone/Getty Images:
24cl, 24cr. Koenigsegg: 7c, 9bl. Denys Kurylow/Shutterstock:
front cover br. Phillip Lange/Shutterstock: 7t. Martin Lehmann/
Shutterstock: 2, 13c. Teddy Leung/Shutterstock: 26cl. I4icocl2/
Shutterstock: 11t. littleng/Shutterstock: 13b. Doug Lin/
Shutterstock: 18t. Svetlana Lukienko/Shutterstock: 8b. makuromi/
Shutterstock: 14c. midnight bird/wikimedia commons: 13t.
Natursports/Shutterstock: 3tr, 14b. Dmitry Naumov/Shutterstock:
5br. PA/PA Images: 11b. Bryon Palmer/Shutterstock: 3tl, 14tr.
Vadim Petrakov/Shutterstock: 16t. Photodynamx/Dreamstime:
front cover bc. Pix-xl/Shutterstock: 8t. Racing One/SC Archive/
Getty Images: 11c. Aizar Raldes/Getty Images: 22tr. betto
rodrigues/Shutterstock: 27t. Mark Sanden/Getty Images: 24t. Luis
Santos/Shutterstock: 15bc. Oskar Schuler/Shutterstock: 25tr.
Sothebys: 12b. SP-Photo/Shutterstock: 5t. Cameron Spencer/
Getty Images: 9c. stevemart/Shutterstock: front cover bl. Studio la
Photography/Shutterstock: 25tl. sumire8/Shutterstock: 14tl, 30b. T
FoxFoto/Shutterstock: 5b. theconstantramble.com: 22tl. Stanislaw
Tokarski/Shutterstock: 26cr. Claudio Villa/Getty Images: 1, 7b,
30tl. Miro Vrlik/Shutterstock: 23t. Wikimedia Commons: 12c, 21tl,
21tr. Vanda Wolff Images/Shutterstock: 6b, 30tr. VenomGT: 17b.
Konstantin Yolshin/Shutterstock: 15bl. Alex Zarubin/Dreamstime:
17c. zygotehassnobrain/Shutterstock: 26cl.

Every attempt has been made to clear copyright.
Should there be any inadvertent omission please apply
to the publisher for rectification.

Dewey number 629'.046
HB ISBN 978 1 4451 4163 3
Library ebook ISBN 978 1 4451 2763 7

Printed in China

MIX
Paper from
responsible sources
FSC
www.fsc.org
FSC® C104740

Franklin Watts
An imprint of
Hachette Children's Group
Part of The Watts Publishing Group
Carmelite House
50 Victoria Embankment
London EC4Y 0DZ

An Hachette UK Company
www.hachette.co.uk

www.franklinwatts.co.uk

Tameside Libraries	
3 8016 0200 3294	
PETERS	12-Jan-2016
J629.22	£12.99
HYD	

CONTENTS

Introduction

Did you just hear a sort of creaky groaning noise? That's because this book is absolutely bursting with information about cars. In it you'll discover essential facts about fast cars, expensive cars, steam-powered cars, Formula One cars and the world's smallest cars. You'll find out...

- Which car to buy when you win the Lottery
- About a car with jet engines
- Where to go on the best road trips

As well as facts and stats, there are quizzes to test your car knowledge. In fact, let's have one now. Before you start reading the book, see if you can answer these questions:

1) What's the world's fastest production car?

2) What does an accelerator do?

3) Where is the longest road in the world?

Read on to find out if you're right.

Prepare to stuff your brain with hundreds of amazing facts and statistics until it's ready to explode! (Actually, we should point out here that the publishers take no responsibility whatsoever for exploding brains.)

CRAZY CAR WORLD VITAL STATISTICS

BACK IN THE NINETEENTH CENTURY, PEOPLE TRAVELLED ON HORSES, BICYCLES OR THEIR OWN TWO FEET. TODAY, FOLLOWING THE INVENTION OF THE INTERNAL COMBUSTION ENGINE, CARS REV THEIR ENGINES AND ZOOM DOWN THE ROAD IN A GREAT BIG HURRY...

STAT ATTACK!

Number of cars on the planet: well over 1 billion (that's one thousand times a million)

Length of road throughout the world: more than 64 million km

Pollution: more than a tenth of greenhouse gas emissions in Europe are caused by cars

Number of road traffic deaths per year worldwide: 1.24 million

Five Cars That Cost More Than a MILLION DOLLAR$

As you cruise through the Caribbean in your luxury superyacht, you're probably wondering what to do with all that spare cash stuffed under your bed. Here are five of the most expensive cars ever, to give you some ideas. There are more mega-expensive cars on pages 9 and 17–19.

1 1963 Ferrari 250 GTO

This red vintage Ferrari, sold in a private sale, achieved the highest price ever for a car. And it's not even new! While your average second-hand family car goes down in value, classic cars like this one can increase to dizzying sums. You'll have to track down the buyer and see if they'll accept an offer.

STAT ATTACK PRICE! US $52 million

2 1962 Ferrari 250 GTO

In 2014, another Ferrari 250 GTO sold for a staggering sum of money. It's the most expensive car ever sold at auction.

STAT ATTACK PRICE! US $34.65 million

③ 1954 Mercedes Benz W196

This car sold at an auction in 2013. Driven by the famous racing driver Juan Manuel Fangio (see page 24), it won the French Grand Prix in 1954.

STAT ATTACK PRICE! US $17.5 million

④ Koenigsegg CCXR Trevita

There are plenty of other mega-expensive classic cars, but if you're really after a brand-new car you might like the Keonigsegg Trevita, the world's most expensive production car. Compared to the classic ones it looks like a bargain.

STAT ATTACK PRICE! US $4.85 million

⑤ Lamborghini Veneno

This roadster is madly expensive to buy new, but since there aren't many of them around and some people just have too much money, second-hand ones are even more expensive!

STAT ATTACK PRICE! US $4.5 million
(or $7.4 million second-hand)

MILLION DOLLAR QUIZ

1 Which racing driver **won the French Grand Prix in 1954 driving the Mercedes that sold at auction for $17.5 million in 2013?**

a) Ayrton Senna

b) Stirling Moss

c) Juan Manuel Fangio

d) Pierre Veyron

2 What was the cost **of the most expensive car ever sold?**

a) $3.6 million

b) $36 million

c) $5.2 million

d) $52 million

3 What type of car **was the most expensive ever sold at auction?**

a) 1962 Ferrari

b) 1930 Mercedes

c) 1926 Rolls Royce

d) 2014 Lamborghini

4 What is the name **of the world's most expensive production car?**

a) Lamborghini Veneno Roadster

b) Koenigsegg CCXR Trevita

c) Pagani Zonda Cinque

d) Maybach Exelero

★ Pricey **answers on page 30**

Three Exclusive Cars

Some luxury cars are only made in limited numbers (editions), so that there aren't many of them about. After all, just think how awful it would be to park your luxury supercar at the supermarket only to find you were parking next to one that's exactly the same! There's another reason for limited editions – there aren't many people in the world who can afford them.

Maybach Exelero

This car really is exclusive. Only one of them was ever made!

STAT ATTACK!

Price: £5.1 million

Number of cars produced: 1

Koenigsegg CCXR Trevita

This is in the mega expensive list on page 7. You'll just have to accept that two other people own one of these.

STAT ATTACK!

Price: £3.1 million

Number of cars produced: 3

Pagani Zonda Cinque

Cinque is Italian for 'five', and that's how many of these cars were made. If you cough up another few hundred thousand pounds, you can have the roofless version, Pagani Zonda Roadster – and only five of them were made too.

STAT ATTACK!

Price: £1 million
(£1.3 million for the Roadster)

Number of cars produced: 5

4 STEAM-POWERED CARS

What, really? Oh yes.

Cars with steam engines once performed better than cars with petrol or diesel engines. In fact, one of them puffed its way to setting a speed record that stood for 100 years, and steam cars are still around today!

Here are some of the best.

1 Fardier á Vapeur

The first ever car was steam powered, built by Nicolas-Joseph Cugnot in 1769. 'Fardier á vapeur' means 'steam cart' – a fardier was an especially big horse-drawn car for moving heavy loads. Cugnot built several versions of his machine, which was huge, slow, bulky and needed constant refuelling. It didn't go far.

The Runabout

The Runabout was the first steam-powered car available to buy. It was produced between 1899 and 1903. A Runabout made in 1900 was sold at auction in 2014 for £31,500!

Stanley Steamer Rocket

The Stanley Steamer Rocket was small, sleek and stream-lined, and went all the way to setting a land-speed record in 1906. It raced along at 204 kph! As a speed record for a steam-powered car, the Rocket's record stood for more than 100 years, until...

Inspiration

Steam-powered cars had almost disappeared by the 1920s. The type of engine most cars use today, the internal combustion engine, had taken over because it was smaller and more efficient. BUT steam enthusiasts carried on driving steam cars – and in 2009 one of them finally broke the land-speed record for a steam-powered car set by the Stanley Steamer Rocket. The car, called the Inspiration, was 7.6 m long and weighed 3 tonnes. It steamed into the record books at an average speed of 225 kph. Even after 100 years the record was only broken by 21 kph!

Five of the World's (Smallest) Cars

Back in the 1950s and 60s, people were trying to stuff themselves into the smallest vehicles they possibly could.

These are the some of the smallest cars in the world that have been manufactured and sold. Some micro-car fans have also made their own roadworthy cars that are even smaller than this, though.

In fact, the one that holds the Guinness World Record was made by Austin Coulson in Arizona, USA – it's just 635 mm high, 655 mm wide and 1260 mm long. There are toy cars bigger than that!

There are small modern production cars too, but none as small as the miniscule models of the olden days (see pages 28–29 for tiny modern electric cars).

1 PEEL P50

The Peel P50 was designed and made in the UK in the 1960s, and still holds the world record for the smallest production car. It can only carry the driver, and has just one door and one headlight. Peel P50s are still being produced today.

STAT ATTACK!

Length: 1,371 mm	
Width: 1,041 mm	
Height: 1,200 mm	
Weight: up to 110 kg	
Top speed: 45 kph (petrol) or 50 kph (electric)	

2 ESHELMAN ADULT SPORT CAR

This tiny open-topped 1950s car looked a bit like a golf cart and needed to be pulled by a rope to start it. To stop it the driver had to reach into the engine casing to flip a switch. There was also a children's version!

STAT ATTACK!

Length: 1,600 mm	
Width: 910 mm	
Height: 810 mm	
Weight: up to 175 kg	
Top speed: 48 kph	

③ THE MIVALINO

Mivalinos were Italian versions of the Messershmitt KR175, a two-seater flip-top car that also came in a sports version (which in this case just means they didn't have roofs). They were built in the 1950s.

STAT ATTACK!

Length: 2,820 mm

Width: 1,220 mm

Height: 1,200 mm

Weight: 220 kg

Top speed: 90 kph

④ HEINKEL KABINE

Heinkel Kabines were 1950s micro-cars designed in Germany and made in Ireland. They were also produced in the UK in the 1960s, where they were known as Trojan 200s.

STAT ATTACK!

Length: 2,500 mm

Width: 1,370 mm

Height: 1,320 mm

Weight: 250 kg

Top speed: 87 kph

⑤ THE ISETTA

These titchy cars were designed in the 1950s and became known as 'bubble cars' because of their shape. A driver and a passenger, and even the shopping, could fit in. Isettas were made under licenses in different countries so they varied a bit – these dimensions are for the Velam Isetta made in France.

STAT ATTACK!

Length: 2,380 mm

Width: 1,420 mm

Height: 1,320 mm

Weight: 350 kg

Top speed: 80 kph

CAR PARTS QUIZ

Use the Internet to help research the answers to these questions.

1 Which of these controls a car's speed?

a) Indicator

b) Accelerator

c) Speedometer

d) Terminator

2 Why do car tyres **have a pattern of grooves on the surface?**

a) To make the car go faster

b) To help with steering the car

c) To make the car stick to the road better

d) All of the above

3 What does a car's odometer **measure?**

a) Speed

b) Fuel level

c) Distance travelled

d) Kilometres per litre of fuel

4 What does a turbocharger **do?**

a) It's a car's battery

b) It helps the car's braking system

c) It's a safety feature

d) It increases the engine's power

5 How many gears **does a Formula One car have?**

a) Two forward and one reverse

b) Four forward and one reverse

c) Eight forward and one reverse

d) Twelve forward gears, no reverse

Mechanical answers **on page 30**

FIVE CAR INVENTIONS WE COULDN'T DO WITHOUT

Invention 1: STEERING WHEEL

Hang on, how can a car not have a steering wheel? Actually the very earliest cars used tillers, like the ones used to steer boats. The first record of a steering wheel was in a Paris to Rouen race, when Alfred Vacheron used a wheel to turn his car.

STAT ATTACK!

Who: Alfred Vacheron

When: 1894

Invention 2: WINDSCREEN WIPERS

Drivers struggled to see through rain-pelted windscreens until Mary Anderson made driving a lot safer by inventing windscreen wipers. The driver had to operate the wipers by hand with a lever – you couldn't just flick a switch.

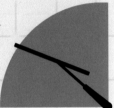

STAT ATTACK!

Who: Mary Anderson

When: 1903

Invention 3: HEADLIGHTS

At first, early cars used gas lights if they were driving at night, but the first electric headlights were switched on in 1898. They needed a lot of improvement to make them reliable, and in 1912 Cadillac produced much better ones.

STAT ATTACK!

Who: Electric Vehicle Company

When: 1898

Invention 4: TRAFFIC LIGHTS

Probably a bit fed up with directing traffic, a policeman called Lester Wire invented the first electric traffic lights. They controlled traffic in Salt Lake City, USA.

STAT ATTACK!

Who: Lester Wire

When: 1912

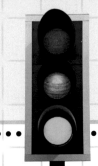

Invention 5: CAT'S EYES

Driving at night on twisty country roads could be perilous before the invention of cat's eyes – studs in the road that reflect light like a cat's eyes do. They show the layout of the road clearly, even in fog.

STAT ATTACK!

Who: Percy Shaw

When: 1935

The World's FOUR Longest Roads

If you ever decide to go on a long road trip, either end of one of these highways might be a good place to start.

① The Pan-American Highway

This road holds the world record for the longest drivable road. It runs all the way from North America down through South America (apart from a gap of 100 km where it stops to make way for the rainforest) and spans a total of 18 countries.

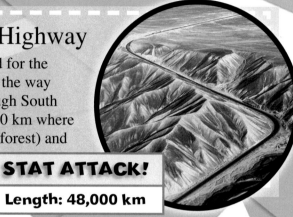

STAT ATTACK!

Length: 48,000 km

② Highway 1

Highway 1 in Australia is a network of roads that go all the way around the edge of the Australian continent. It's the world's longest national road (the Pan-American highway runs through different countries), and over 1 million people travel on it every day.

STAT ATTACK!

Length: 14,500 km

③ Trans-Siberian Highway

The Trans-Siberian highway is made up of seven different roads, and runs from St Petersburg in the west of Russia all the way to Vladivostok on the Pacific coast.

STAT ATTACK!

Length: 11,000 km

④ Trans-Canada Highway

The second-longest national highway in the world, the Trans-Canada, spans all ten Canadian provinces, linking Canada's major cities. It runs from Victoria in British Columbia to St John's City in Newfoundland and Labrador.

STAT ATTACK!

Length: 7,821 km

6 Super fast Supercars

That Go Faster Than 400 kph

Unlike racing cars, these high-velocity vehicles can legally be driven on the road. And all of them can whizz along at over 400 kph! That really is crazy. Keep your eyes peeled and you might spot one – but blink and you'll miss it.

1

Bugatti Veyron 16.4 Grand Sport Vitesse

At the moment, this is the world's fastest production car (but it could be overtaken any second now). The Veyron is named after Pierre Veyron, a super-speedy French racing driver from the early 20th century.

STAT ATTACK!

Top speed: 431 kph
0-100 kph: 2.5 seconds
Engine capacity: 7,993 cc
Brake horsepower: 1,200
Release date: 2010
Price: £1.7 million

2

Hennessey Venom GT

The Venom set a world record for 0-300 kph in 13.63 seconds. Its top speed is reported to be 435.2 kph, though the Bugatti Veyron still holds the official Guinness World Record.

STAT ATTACK!

Top speed: 435.2 kph (unofficial)
0-60 kph: 2.5 seconds
Engine capacity: 6,200 cc
Brake horsepower: 1,244
Release date: 2010
Price: £1.2 million

3

✸ Koenigsegg Agera R ✸

This car holds the Guinness World Record for the fastest time from 0-300 kph – 21.19 seconds, though it's not the fastest from 0-100. It also claims to have a faster top speed than the Bugatti Veyron.

STAT ATTACK!

Top speed: 440 kph (unoffical)	
0-100 kph: 2.9 seconds	
Engine capacity: 5,000 cc	
Brake horsepower: 1,100	
Release date: 2011	
Price: £1 million	

4

✸ 9ff GT9 R ✸

It's not a very catchy name, is it? The car is a modified Porsche, made by German tuning company 9ff.

STAT ATTACK!

Top speed: 414 kph – claimed	
0-100 km/h: 2.9 seconds	
Engine capacity: 4,000 cc	
Brake horsepower: 1,120	
Release date: 2009	
Price: £540,000	

5

✸ SSC* Ultimate Aero TT ✸

This car was the fastest in the world from 2007 to 2010. 'Aero' doesn't mean it can fly – it refers to the car's aerodynamic design.

STAT ATTACK!

Top speed: 413 kph	
0-100 km/h: 2.7 seconds	
Engine capacity: 6,200 cc	
Brake horsepower: 1,287	
Release date: 2007	
Price: £405,662	

*formerly ShelbySuperCars Inc.

✳ Dauer 962 LM ✳

The 'LM' stands for Le Mans, one of the oldest and fastest race tracks in the world. A racing version of this car won at Le Mans in 1994.

STAT ATTACK!

Top speed: 404 kph
0-100 kph: 2.6 seconds
Engine capacity: 2,994 cc
Brake horsepower: 730
Release date: 1993
Price: £750,000

✴ The Land-speed ✴ Record-breaking Car

Land-speed records have been made and broken since 1898 (the first one reached 63.15 kph). The current record holder is Thrust SSC (SSC stands for supersonic car). In 1997 it zoomed across the Black Rock Desert, USA at a blistering 1,228 kph, breaking the land-speed record and the sound barrier. The car's two huge Rolls Royce Spey engines are bigger than the rest of the car put together, and needed 55 litres of fuel to cover 1 km. A new car, the Bloodhound SSC, aims to break the land-speed record. Visit http://www.bloodhoundssc.com.

1,228 kph

EARLY CARS QUIZ

Use the Internet to help research the answers to these questions.

1 **Which** safety feature **invented in 1885 was made compulsory to use in the UK in 1983?**

a) Air bags   **b)** Seat belts

c) Bumpers   **d)** Fog lights

2 **Whose** famous factory **produced the first mass-produced, affordable cars?**

a) Ramsom E Olds   **b)** Gottlieb Daimler

c) Karl Benz   **d)** Henry Ford

3 **The** first car **to go faster than 100 kph was powered by which of the following?**

a) Electricity   **b)** Petrol

c) Steam   **d)** Diesel

4 **What did** Charles Goodyear **invent that kept cars rolling?**

a) Hard-wearing rubber   **b)** Steering wheels

c) A battery   **d)** A more efficient engine

5 **In 1865, the UK**'s 'Red Flag Act' **made drivers do which of the following?**

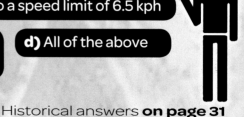

a) Have three operators   **b)** Keep to a speed limit of 6.5 kph

c) Have someone walk in front of the car waving a red flag as a warning   **d)** All of the above

Historical answers **on page 31**

4 Fantastic Female *** Racing Drivers

Driving racing cars isn't just for the boys – oh no!

Women have been zooming around chicanes for decades.
These are some of the best women racing drivers of all time.

1 LOUISE SMITH

Louise Smith was a female racing driver pioneer. She became known as the First Lady of NASCAR – (the National Association of Stock Car Auto Racing in the United States). Smith saw her first NASCAR race in 1949 and straight away felt she had to enter – so she raced her family's car. She continued to race until 1956, and won 38 races.

2 LELLA LOMBARDI

Italian Lella Lombardi was a Formula One driver and the only woman to be placed in the first six in a World Championship race. She raced in the 1970s, and took part in 17 World Championship Grand Prix, more than any other female driver.

3 DESIRÉ WILSON

In 1980, Desiré Wilson (centre) from South Africa became the only woman to win a Formula One race. She won the race at Brands Hatch, and a grandstand at the race track was named after her in honour of her achievement.

4 DANICA PATRICK

Danica Patrick is currently the world's most successful woman in American racing. She came third in the Indianapolis 500 in 2009, the highest place ever for a woman, and won the Indy Japan 300, the only win for a woman in an Indycar series race.

FOUR OF THE WORLD'S MOST DANGEROUS ROADS

Driving can be dangerous on the best of roads, so imagine the hazards when you're perched on the edge of a canyon or navigating a hostile wilderness.

1 ☠ NORTH YUNGAS ROAD, BOLIVIA

Snaking its way along a mountainside, the North Yungas Road has a terrifying reputation as the most dangerous road in the world. If cars try to pass one another, they're just centimetres away from a 600-metre drop. It's also known as Death Road, because according to estimates between 200 and 300 people die on it each year.

2 ☠ JAMES DALTON HIGHWAY, ALASKA

Cutting across a frozen wilderness in the middle of nowhere, this pot-holed road is scoured by vicious, icy winds that sometimes carry stones. Break down, blow a tyre or shatter your windscreen here and you're miles away from help.

3 ☠ CALIFORNIA STATE ROUTE 138

Sections of this road in southern California are narrow, winding and cling to the side of the San Bernardino Mountains. Passing can be extremely hazardous, and the road has earned a reputation as one of the most dangerous in America.

4

☠ EYRE HIGHWAY

This road cuts across the Nullarbor Plain, a hot, dry desert in southern Australia. Eyre is perilous because it's so straight and flat that drivers have to work hard to stay alert. If they lose concentration and have an accident, they're in the middle of a desert which is baking hot by day or freezing cold at night.

TOP 3 HYBRID CARS

Drivers who want to reduce pollution, but don't want to hang around waiting for an electric car to recharge (see pages 28–29), might choose a hybrid car – a cross between a petrol-engine car and an electric car (there are diesel-electric hybrids available too). They cover more kilometres for every litre of fuel, so they're cheaper to run as well as being better for the environment.

These are three of the most popular:

1. Toyota Prius

This was the first mass-produced hybrid car, and more than 3 million of them have been sold, making it the best-selling hybrid too.

STAT ATTACK!

In production since 1997

Latest model fuel economy:
4.4 litres per 100 km

2. Honda Civic

The Civic's engine won the International Engine of the Year for its size for three years from 2002 to 2004, and was the most fuel-efficient for 2003 and 2004.

STAT ATTACK!

In production since 2001

Latest model fuel economy:
5.3 litres per 100 km

3. Ford Fusion

This won 2013 Green Car of the Year because it's environmentally friendly — not because of its paint colour!

STAT ATTACK!

In production since 2009

Latest model fuel economy:
6.0 litres per 100 km

Ayrton Senna

1

The brilliant Brazilian Ayrton Senna raced from 1984, and had 41 Grand Prix wins before his death in 1994, after he crashed during a race.

STAT ATTACK!

World Championship titles: 3

Grand Prix starts: 161

Grand Prix wins: 41

Pole positions: 65

Juan Manuel Fangio

2

Argentinian Fangio was already in his forties when he started Formula One racing in 1951. He drove for seven seasons, but in that short space of time he set standards that made him famous for years to come – he won almost half the Grand Prix races he started.

STAT ATTACK!

World Championship titles: 5

Grand Prix starts: 51

Grand Prix wins: 24

Pole positions: 28

Jim Clark

3

Jim Clark, from Scotland, became world famous in the 1960s, especially after his record 25 Grand Prix wins. He also set a record for pole positions. Clark died in a crash in a Formula Two race in 1968 a few months after his last Grand Prix win in South Africa.

STAT ATTACK!

World Championship titles: 2

Grand Prix starts: 72

Grand Prix wins: 25

Pole positions: 33

Michael Schumacher

4

Schumacher had a long career as a Formula One driver, and during that time he set the world record for the most Grand Prix wins ever: a total of 91 victories. Now that's just showing off. He's also the driver with the longest time span between his first Grand Prix win, in 1992, and his last, in 2006.

STAT ATTACK!

World Championship titles: 7	
Grand Prix starts: 303	
Grand Prix wins: 91	
Pole positions: 68	

Alain Prost

5

French driver Alain Prost competed in the 1980s and 90s, a rival of Ayrton Senna. He held the world record for the most Grand Prix wins until he was overtaken by Michael Schumacher, and still holds second place.

STAT ATTACK!

World Championship titles: 4	
Grand Prix starts: 199	
Grand Prix wins: 51	
Pole positions: 33	

Sebastian Vettel

6

Vettel became the youngest winner of a Grand Prix in 2008 when he was just 21. He also holds the record for the highest number of Grand Prix wins in a row: nine, in the 2013 season.

STAT ATTACK!

World Championship titles: 4	
Grand Prix starts: 139	
Grand Prix wins: 39	
Pole positions: 45	

Three Best-selling Cars

We've found out about cars that cost millions, or reach stomach-churning speeds, or are so exclusive that only one or two have ever been made. But what about the cars that most people drive – **the kind that might be your family's car . . .**

Toyota Corolla

This brand has been going since 1966, though it's been through lots of design changes since then. It became the world's best-selling car in 1974. Millions of Toyota Corollas have been sold. The car also holds the world record for the highest number of total sales in a single year – 1.36 million Corollas were sold in 2005.

STAT ATTACK!

Number of cars sold:
More than 39 million

VW Beetle

The Volkswagon Beetle was designed as a simple, cheap and economical car for ordinary people. It was so popular that it kept the same basic design from 1938 until 2003, when it had a bit of a makeover.
It holds the world record for the best-selling single model of any car.

STAT ATTACK!

Number of cars sold:
More than 21.5 million

Model T Ford

The Ford Model T was produced between 1908 and 1927 in Henry Ford's factories, which used fast-paced production lines to get the cars made cheaply and efficiently. From 1915 to 1925, Model Ts only came in one colour: black, because it was the paint colour that dried the quickest! The cars were simple but practical. People liked them, and more Model Ts were sold than any other type of car at that time.

STAT ATTACK!

Number of cars sold:
More than 15 million

✴ CAR MAKERS QUIZ ✴

Use the Internet to help research the answers to these questions.

1 **Which of these** car manufacturers' mascot **is a rearing horse?**

a) Ford   **b)** Mercedes

c) Ferrari   **d)** Alpha Romeo

2  **Which make of car does** James Bond **traditionally drive?**

a) Aston Martin   **b)** Rolls Royce

c) Bentley   **d)** Porsche

3 **Which car maker produces the** Fiesta, Focus **and** Mondeo**?**

✴ focus ✴

a) Vauxhall   **b)** Toyota

c) BMW   **d)** Ford

4 **Which of these** car makers' logos **isn't circular?**

a) Vauxhall

b) Nissan

c) Jaguar

d) Mercedes

5 **Which car maker has a** bull **on its logo?**

a) Peugeot   **b)** Lamborghini

c) Citroen   **d)** Renault

Manufactured answers **on page 31**

5 ELECTRIC CARS

Some early cars ran on electricity, but petrol and diesel engines proved more popular. Emissions from these engines smell horrible and pollute the air. Plus the fossil fuels they run on will eventually run out. So now electric cars are back in fashion, and although they still take a while to recharge between trips, they're getting better and better (and smaller and smaller) . . .

1 BOLLORÉ BLUECAR

This French electric car can travel a fair distance before it needs recharging, then a quick two-hour charge will top it up to half its full capacity.

STAT ATTACK!

Range: 250 km	
Top speed: 135 kph	
Time for full recharge: 6 hours	

2 KANDI COCO

This sweet sounding Chinese electric car is only 2.63 m long and 1.55 m wide.

STAT ATTACK!

Range: 64 km	
Top speed: 80 kph	
Time for full recharge: 6 hours	

3 ELBIL NORGE BUDDY CAR

This Norwegian car is even smaller than the Kandi Coco – only 2.44 m long.

STAT ATTACK!

Range: 60 km	
Top speed: 80 kph	
Time for full recharge: 6–8 hours	

4 THE TANGO

The Tango is so narrow that some motorbikes are wider – it's 99 cm wide. Despite that it can carry two people, one behind the other. It leans into corners like a motorbike.

STAT ATTACK!

Range: 60–240 km	
Top speed: 240 kph	
Time for full recharge: 3 hours	

5 LUMENEO SMERA

This French two-seater car is narrower still at just 96 cm, and also leans into curves.

STAT ATTACK!

Range: 100 km	
Top speed: 110 kph	
Time for full recharge: 4 hours	

Quiz Answers

MILLION DOLLAR QUIZ ANWER (PAGE 8)

 1c

 2d

3a

4b

$ 1 0 0 0 0 0 0

CAR PARTS QUIZ ANSWERS (PAGE 14)

1b

2c) the grooves in the rubber prevent the tyres from slipping.

3c

4d

5c

EARLY CARS QUIZ ANSWERS (PAGE 20)

1b

2d) Ford's production line could build a car in 90 minutes, which made the cars much more affordable.

3a) The first car to exceed 100 kph was Camille Jenatzy's electric La Jamais Contente in 1899. Electric cars took a long time to recharge, so petrol-powered vehicles took over.

4a) In 1839 Charles Goodyear invented a hard-wearing rubber that could be used on car tyres, and the first solid rubber tyre was produced in 1846. Air-filled rubber tyres weren't produced until 1895.

5d) There wasn't much point in driving a car at all! The act was withdrawn in 1896, and the speed limit was increased to 22 kph.

CAR MAKERS QUIZ ANSWERS (PAGE 27)

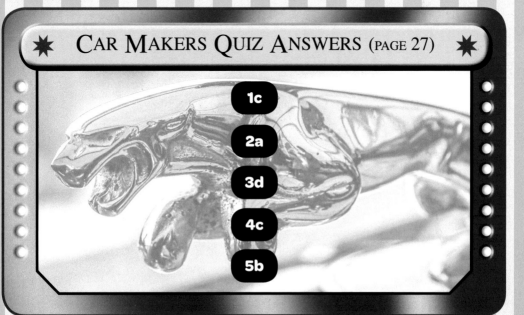

1c

2a

3d

4c

5b

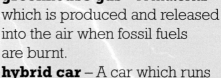

aerodynamic – Having a shape which reduces the drag from air moving past a solid object, such as a car.

brake horsepower – The actual available power of an engine, often displayed as bhp.

chicane – A sharp double bend on a racing track.

classic car – An often old, high-quality car.

fossil fuel – A natural material formed from the remains of living things, which is burnt to produce energy. Petrol and diesel come from petroleum, which is a fossil fuel.

Grand Prix – An important series of car races held in various countries throughout the year.

greenhouse gas – A material which is produced and released into the air when fossil fuels are burnt.

hybrid car – A car which runs using an internal combustion engine and an electric motor.

internal combustion engine – An engine which generates energy through the burning of fuel mixed with air. The hot gas produced is used to move parts of the engine, such as pistons, which help move the car along.

production car – One of many identical cars for sale to the public and driven on public roads.

roadster – A roofless, two-seater car.

supercar – A very fast, high-quality sports car.

INDEX